My

DEAREST
Future
Spouse

Prayer & Reflection

Nike Joy

Dedication

This book is dedicated to Somebody's Son – MY HUSBAND.

Moreover the word of the Lord came to me, saying:

[9] *"The hands of Zerubbabel have laid the foundation of this temple; His hands shall also finish it. Then you will know that the Lord of hosts has sent Me to you.* [10] *For who has despised the day of small things? For these seven rejoice to see the plumb line in the hand of Zerubbabel. They are the eyes of the Lord, Which scan to and from throughout the whole earth."* *Zechariah 4:8-10*

Acknowledgment

To my loved ones, sisters, spiritual mentors, spiritual mothers, my wise women, my covering, and you reading this – THANK YOU for supporting God's vision and Kingdom work. Thank you for believing the God in me.

About the Author

Nike Joy is a born-again believer. She has been in the mental health field for almost 20 years and enjoys marketplace ministry. She loves to sing and has been singing for several decades. She has dedicated her time to growing others in the word of God and teaching healthy boundaries as well.

She brings the word of God to live and teaches others how to pray and walk effectively in who God has called them to be. She is a natural encourager and light to be around.

Nike serves in her local community and church. She is a member of Alpha Theta Omega Christian Sorority, Incorporated.

Nike Joy

www.nikejoy.com
nikejoyllc@gmail.com

Prayer & Reflection

Each day, you will have space to write down and answer the questions below.

What's going on today? Write down your emotions and why are you feeling this way?

_____

_____

_____

_____

How can I pray for him/her today? (Pray for then and add a scripture maybe scriptures)

_____

_____

_____

_____

Is there anything on my heart I'll like to share with You today?

_____

_____

_____

_____

For my single folks – *why do you want to pray for your spouse?*
Why am I doing this? Where is my faith?

_____

_____

_____

_____

_____

Write down what you truly desire in a spouse. I recommend 3 parts — spiritually, mentally, and physically.

_____

_____

_____

_____

_____

_____

_____

_____

_____

_____

_____

Pray over this list daily. Revisit them each day and ask yourself;

1. *Is this still in alignment with what God is saying to me and showing me?*

_____

_____

_____

_____

_____

_____

_____

2. *Is this person (I'm interested in) in alignment with what God already spoke or showed me?*

_____

_____

_____

_____

_____

_____

_____

_____

_____

_____

For my married, dating, in relationships, engaged folks.

Make sure you do not have ulterior motive more than the desire to see your spouse/person walk closely with God.

Why am I doing this?

_____
_____
_____
_____
_____

Am I truly desiring Godly things for my spouse?

_____
_____
_____
_____
_____

Am I praying so that God can turn my spouse heart to Him or to me?

_____
_____
_____
_____
_____

Before we begin, let us stand in agreement and align our faith properly with God.

Do you believe what you are about to pray for? If not, meditate on Mark 11:24 and 2 Corinthians 4:13. Do not proceed without aligning your faith.

Therefore, I say to you, whatever things you ask when you pray, believe that you receive them, and you will have them. Mark 11:24

And since we have the same spirit of faith, according to what is written, "I believed and therefore I spoke," we also believe and therefore speak. 2 Corinthians 4:13

Why is this important?

We need to make sure that we are not following a plan of prayer just because it feels cute or in style. However, if you are hesitant but you feel like this is what you are being led to do right now. I pray this simple verse over you, "I believe but help my unbelief" Lord.

Strength & Honor

My prayer for you today comes from several scriptures because I love you that much. Joshua 1:5 says no man will ever be able to stand before you all the days of your life. You will be a pillar of strength. Every Goliath before you will fall. You my dear will be like a tree planted by the rivers of water and produces fruits in its season according to Psalm 1:3. You will never be put to shame Psalm 25:2 because God is with you, God will establish you according to 1 Corinthians 1:8. I pray these scriptures over you today. I pray that they will be active, living, and constant in every area of your life. I pray that God will begin to watch over this word to bring it to fruition and accomplishment in your life, in Jesus mighty name, amen.

No man shall be able to stand before You all the days of Your life; as I was with Moses, so I will be with You. I will not leave You nor forsake You. Joshua 1:5

Who will also confirm You to the end, that You may be blameless in the day of our Lord Jesus Christ. 1 Corinthians 1:8

He shall be like a tree planted by the rivers of water, that brings forth its fruit in its season, whose leaf also shall not wither; and whatever he does shall prosper Psalm 1:3

O my God, I trust in You; Let me not be ashamed; Let not my enemies triumph over me. Psalm 25:2

Affirmation: You will be a person of strength and honor.

_____

_____

_____

_____

_____

_____

_____

_____

Psalm 23

Today's prayer comes from Psalm 23. I pray wherever you are today, that God will be the Shepherd over your life. I pray He restores your soul and leads you in the path of righteousness. I pray no matter what valley you're in, you my dearest will fear no evil. I pray He anoints your head with oil and Your cup overflows. I pray His goodness and mercy follows you all the days of your life, in Jesus name, amen.

The Lord is my shepherd; I shall not want. ² He makes me to lie down in green pastures; He leads me beside the still waters. ³ He restores my soul; He leads me in the paths of righteousness for His name's sake. ⁴ Yea, though I walk through the valley of the shadow of death, I will fear no evil; for You are with me; Your rod and Your staff, they comfort me. ⁵ You prepare a table before me in the presence of my enemies; You anoint my head with oil; my cup runs over. ⁶ Surely goodness and mercy shall follow me all the days of my life; and I will dwell in the house of the Lord forever. Psalm 23

Affirmation: You will be led by God throughout your life.

Strong & Courageous

Lord Jesus, I thank You for my love. I thank God because He is giving you the desire to be more like Him daily. I ask that God will grow and increase you in confidence and trust in Him. That you will be reminded of the great things God has done before and reassure you that He is more than able to do great things in your life again. Joshua 1:9 commands them to be strong and courageous in You God. I pray for you this day, that He will bring godly boldness out of you. That you will walk in God's strength and not your own. I thank God for watching over you this day and days to come, in Jesus name, amen.

Have I not commanded you? Be strong and courageous. Do not be frightened, and do not be dismayed, for the Lord your God is with you wherever you go." Joshua 1:9

Affirmation: You will be walk in courage and not fear all the days of your life.

Heart of God

Lord God, I thank You for Your special delivery and the gift they are in all facets of life. I thank God for keeping you in Him. I am grateful for creating and designing us for one another. I pray that you know that Jesus is your everything. I pray you lead a life of a person after God's own heart according to Acts 13:22. I pray that you will know that you are created to walk according to God's heart and will and that you will continue to do all He has commanded of you, in Jesus name, amen.

And when he had removed him, He raised up David to be their king, of whom He testified and said, 'I have found in David the son of Jesse a man after my heart, who will do all My will.' Acts 13:22

Affirmation: You will walk through life knowing you are chosen by God.

Healing & Closeness

Hey my love, I am praying strength for you today in every area you may feel weak. Psalm 34:18 reminds us that God is near to the brokenhearted and those whose spirits are crushed. I am praying that in all areas that you have experienced brokenness, that God will mend it. I pray God will restore, renew, and replenish you. I pray the healing hand of God will show up in all areas you've encountered pain, hurt, brokenness, disappointment, and shame. I pray you will draw closer to God this day as He draws closer to you according to James 4:8a. I pray you continue to lead a Christ-centered life in Him, in Jesus name, amen.

The Lord is near to the brokenhearted and saves the crushed in spirit. Psalm 35:18
Draw near to God, and He will draw near to you. James 4:8a

Affirmation: You are healed and not a product of your pain.

Discern & Lead

Today's prayer is out of the book of 1 Kings 3:9. Lord will give you - His servant an understanding heart to govern His people, that you will discern between good and evil. I thank God that He has given you the grace to lead with genuineness. Thank You Jesus for calling them to leadership. I pray this day that you will be able to discern what is right from what is wrong as you lead God's people in holiness and godliness in Christ Jesus. I pray that what is right will not depart from you. I pray your discernment will consistently increase and you will be repulsed by what repulses God, in Jesus name, amen.

Give your servant therefore an understanding mind to govern Your people, that I may discern between good and evil, for who is able to govern this Your great people?" 1 Kings 3:9

Affirmation: You will walk in wisdom in leadership.

Supply

I pray that our God Almighty and Heavenly Father shall supply all your needs babe according to His riches in glory by Christ Jesus for you all the days of your life. I pray that you will lack nothing God has for you in this life. I pray you will trust in His supply and resources, as you encounter life's situation. I pray when there's a Red Sea before you and what feels like an Egyptian army behind you, you will trust in God's ability to supply all your needs and path the sea. I pray you will not for a moment live a day or a minute not knowing that God's got you covered in every area of your life. I pray you have the constant knowing and assurance that He is supplying ALL your needs, in Jesus name, amen.

And my God will supply every need of yours according to His riches in glory in Christ Jesus. Philippians 4:19

Affirmation: All you needs will be met in God Almighty.

Fear of God

I am praying this powerful word over you today. That you will live life in reverential fear of the name of the Lord. From the west and His glory from the rising of the sun. My prayer is that when they shall come in like a flood the Spirit of the Lord shall lift up a standard against the enemy in your life and everything that concerns you. I called upon Heaven's army on your behalf today, I lift up the standard of God in your life. I come against every lie and counterfeit that is trying to plague your life and infiltrate your atmosphere. I lift up Heaven's standard on your behalf, in Jesus name, amen.

So they shall fear the name of the Lord from the west, and His glory from the rising of the sun; for He will come like a rushing stream, which the wind of the Lord drives. Isaiah 59:19

Affirmation: You will walk in reverential fear of God.

Newness

My prayer is that God will open your spiritual eyes to see what He's doing in your life and around you. I pray you will perceive His glory knowing that whatever desert you face, you are in, or is before you; you will be rest assured that He will spring forth rivers in the desert and make a way in the wilderness because you are so dear to Him. I pray you walk fully and forever in this promise and assurance, in Jesus name, amen.

Behold, I am doing a new thing; now it springs forth, do you not perceive it? I will make a way in the wilderness and rivers in the desert. Isaiah 43:19

Affirmation: You will see God's work in your life.

God's Purpose & Plan

Lord I thank You for the visionary You have created them to be. That you – my dearest is so innovative. There is so much gifting in you. Proverbs tells us many are the plans in your heart and mind, but I pray for you today that the Lord's is the only one that will stand. I pray that God's purpose for your life will consistently and continually be your heart desires. You will delight in God's purpose for your life in this moment, future, and for the rest of your life. Nothing will be able to stand in place and against God's purpose for you, in Jesus name, amen.

Many are the plans in the mind of a man, but it is the purpose of the Lord that will stand. Proverbs 19:21

Affirmation: You will fulfill God's purpose for your life.

Presence & Peace of God

I pray that the presence of God will go with you and He will give you rest. I pray you will know that He is fighting for you and you will keep your peace. I pray that wherever you are in this moment that you will feel the presence of God is there with you. That your spirit, mind, and body is slowly and well rested in this assurance of God's presence with you. That whatever battle you are facing, you know God is fighting for you and will always fight for you. I pray you rest in this peace from this moment on and forever, in Jesus name, amen.

Exodus 33:14
14 And He said, "My presence will go with you, and I will give you rest."
Exodus 14:14
The Lord will fight for you, and you will keep your peace."

Affirmation: You will live in God's peaceful presence and peace.

Be Transformed

I pray that you my love will not conform to this world. But you are transformed by the renewing of your mind. I pray when you encounter the test of life, you will be able to discern what is the will of God, what is good, and acceptable, and perfect. My prayer for you is that you will not run away from the transformative work of God that He is doing on the inside of you. In this, you will not misstep my love. I pray you will do the continual work to stay grounded in God by the renewing of your mind. I pray you are not carried away by earthly wisdom, intellect, or the ways of man. I pray that your discernment for what is good, acceptable, and perfect will of God will not fail you, in Jesus name, amen.

Do not be conformed to this world, but be transformed by the renewal of your mind, that by testing you may discern what is the will of God, what is good and acceptable and perfect. Romans 12:2

Affirmation: You will walk in God's transformative power all the days of your life.

His Plan & Purpose

My desire for you in prayer today is that the Lord God your Maker has sworn over you saying that, as He has planned for your life- SO SHALL IT BE. As He has purposed for you - SO IT SHALL STAND. I pray that you walk in the confidence of this word every day. I pray you have an unshakable knowing that God's plans over your life shall be and that everything he has purpose for you shall stand. Nothing can hinder or stop His plan and purpose for your life. Go ahead babe and walk confidently in God's plans and purposes for your life knowing you cannot be stopped, in Jesus name, amen.

The Lord of hosts has sworn: "As I have planned, so shall it be, and as I have purposed, so shall it stand. Isaiah 14:24

Affirmation: God's purpose and plan for your life will stand.

Establish me Oh Lord

My love, I pray for you in this day that you will be established in Christ Jesus righteousness. You shall be far and free from oppression, and you shall not fear. No terror shall come near you, your dwelling, and all that concerns you. I pray whatever assembles against you in strife is not of God and for your sake my love – they will all fall. I pray you are confident and know it is not of God. Whoever and whatever comes against you shall definitely fall for your sake. Because of God's covering over your life, nothing that a assembles against you will stand because you are rooted and standing in Christ Jesus - your firm foundation, in Jesus name, amen.

In righteousness you shall be established; you shall be far from oppression, for you shall not fear; and from terror, for it shall not come near you. [15] If anyone stirs up strife, it is not from me; whoever stirs up strife with you shall fall because of you. Isaiah 54:14-15

Affirmation: You are established in God's righteousness.

Protection from weapons & tongues

I so so so love this scripture for your life. I am praying this over your life from this moment and for the rest of your life. I pray that no weapon(s) formed against you will prosper and everything tongue that rise up against you in judgment shall be condemned. Guess what honey, this is your heritage as the servant of the Lord and your righteousness is of Him. Jesus I pray over Your precious child that no matter what they encounter or forms against them, they will rest in Your promises that though they may form they will never prosper. Though the tongues may rise in judgment against you, you shall never be condemned because it is their God-given right here on earth righteously, in Jesus name, amen.

no weapon that is fashioned against you shall succeed, and you shall refute every tongue that rises against you in judgment. This is the heritage of the servants of the Lord and their vindication from me, declares the Lord." Isaiah 54:17

Affirmation: You will walk in your Godly heritage.

Love is...

This powerful word reminds me that God loves you – my dearest. I pray that the love in your heart is modeled after that in 1 Corinthians 13 and it will withstand the trials of life. I pray your love is kind and does not envy, does not parade itself, and is not puffed up. I pray the love you're walking in does not behave rudely, does not seek its own and self-gain, it is not easily provoked, and thinks no evil. I pray this will be your daily portion in God. I pray God's unadulterated love over your life. I pray your love and passion for others will not be abused and misused. I pray your will have wisdom and use discernment in how to dispense love without holding back. You will not allow the hurt of the world to darken the light that comes with the love in your heart, in Jesus name, amen.

Love is patient and kind; love does not envy or boast; it is not arrogant [5] or rude. It does not insist on its own way; it is not irritable or resentful; [6] it does not rejoice at wrongdoing, but rejoices with the truth. 1 Corinthians 13:4-6

Affirmation: You will know you are loved and walk in love.

_____

_____

_____

_____

_____

_____

_____

_____

_____

Check in…

We are almost midway through this.
How is your faith?
Where is your faith?
Are you still trusting and believing?

Let us stand in agreement and align our faith properly with God AGAIN. Wherever you stand in your faith, let's meditate on Mark 11:24 and 2 Corinthians 4:13.

Therefore, I say to You, whatever things You ask when You pray, believe that You receive them, and You will have them. Mark 11:24

And since we have the same spirit of faith, according to what is written, "I believed and therefore I spoke," we also believe and therefore speak. 2 Corinthians 4:13

Why is this important?

In case you have been breezing through this, I want us to use this moment to slow down and meditate on what you have read so far. If you have been taking your time through this – that is perfectly OK as well.

We just want to make sure our hearts are in the right place with God.

Teach me to War & Battle

Hey Battle Axe, I am still praying for you. I pray that you will lean into what God is saying to you and asking of you. I am grateful that you are a person of valor and great stature. I pray that you will lean on God today as the Rock of your life. That you would allow Him to train your hands for war and your fingers to do battle. I pray in this season of your life, you will not pray amiss. I pray you will be Holy Spirit led in your prayer life, in your devotional life, and all that you do. I pray that there will be outward manifestation of your daily time with the Lord as He teaches you to war and battle in His name, amen.

Blessed be the Lord, my rock, who trains my hands for war, and my fingers for battle; Psalm 144:11

Affirmation: You will fight the good fight of faith and win.

Love for God

I pray you shall love the Lord your God with all your heart, with all your soul, with all your strength, and with all your mind, and love your neighbor as yourself. I pray that the outward love you exude will be a manifestation of your internal dedication to the things of God and love for His people. I pray nothing will stand between you and your love for God and things that concerns Him. I pray His love, will, and promises will constantly be your heart's desire. I pray nothing you desire or is presented to you will separate you from this promise in His word, in Jesus name, amen.

And he answered, "You shall love the Lord your God with all your heart and with all your soul and with all your strength and with all your mind, and your neighbor as yourself." Luke 10:27

Affirmation: You will ALWAYS walk in love and purity in God.

Trust in God

I am running out of cute names to call you – my dearest.

I am praying for you that all your trust will be placed in God. I pray that your intellect will not hinder you from relying solely on Him in all areas of your life. I pray that you will be greatly and exceedingly blessed for putting your trust in God. I pray your obedience and sacrifice to the things of God and trust in Him will allow you to walk tall without remorse. I pray that this blessedness is a revealing of your steadfastness and His presence and living a life of consecration not in your own strength but in Him, in Jesus name, amen.

"Blessed is the man who trusts in the Lord whose trust is the Lord. Jeremiah 17:7

Affirmation: You will put your trust in God and you are blessed.

Wisdom

I pray for you that you will walk in wisdom and not folly all the days of your life. I pray that you will listen to wise counsel. I pray you will not allow insults and things contrary to the will of God for you not penetrate your heart. I pray you will walk in truthfulness and not be an abomination to God. I pray you will walk and act faithfully. I pray you will walk prudently before God and in knowledge. I pray you will live this out in every area of your life and every moment of your life with diligence, in Jesus name, amen.

Proverbs 22
15 *The way of a fool is right in his own eyes,*
   but a wise man listens to advice.
16 *The vexation of a fool is known at once,*
   but the prudent ignores an insult.
22 *Lying lips are an abomination to the Lord,*
   but those who act faithfully are his delight.
23 *A prudent man conceals knowledge,*
   but the heart of fools proclaims folly.

Affirmation: You will walk in wisdom as a prudent man.

Kingdom Seeker

This is another one of my favorites for you. I pray that you will seek first the Kingdom of God and His righteousness in all that you do. I pray that you will do so with assurance knowing that everything you need is provided. It is my heart's desire and prayer for you that your longing and heart cry will be to seek first the Kingdom of God daily. My prayer is that you will walk in righteousness in a steadfast manner. Because of this steadfastness, you will lack nothing in your life. That nothing will be missing or withheld from you, in Jesus name, amen.

But seek first the kingdom of God and His righteousness, and all these things will be added to you. Matthew 6:33

Affirmation: You will desire to put God first.

Increase in God

I pray that your love may abound and increase in knowledge of things of God and in discernment. I pray that your life will showcase the excellence of God and you will lead a life blameless and pure before God. Not a life of perfection but you will do according to His will and good pleasure to live a spotless life. I pray you remain and be filled with the fruits of righteousness in sincerity without offense till the day of Jesus Christ, to His glory and praise of God, in Jesus name, amen.

And it is my prayer that your love may abound more and more, with knowledge and all discernment, [10] so that you may approve what is excellent, and so be pure and blameless for the day of Christ, [11] filled with the fruit of righteousness that comes through Jesus Christ, to the glory and praise of God. Philippians 1:9-11

Affirmation: You will see increase all the days of your life.

Godly Direction

My prayer for you is that as you walk through life and in all that you do, you will hear the voice of the Lord. I pray you will not miss His voice behind you speaking to you. You will hear Him telling you where to walk, when to turn right, when to turn left, and you will be obedient in this. I pray you will walk in obedience in guidance of the Lord and His directing voice. His powerful hands will never depart from you. I pray there will be no moment in your life that you do not hear His direction moving you towards Him and as He is destined for you. I pray you will continually have a servant's heart – a heart to walk in obedience towards God's instructions for your life, in Jesus name, amen.

And your ears shall hear a word behind you, saying, "This is the way, walk in it," when you turn to the right or when you turn to the left. Isaiah 30:21

Affirmation: You will be led by God.

Desire for God

My prayer for you today is that you will thirst after the things of God. I pray as the deer pants for Water Brooks, so will your soul pants after God. I pray that nothing in life will be able to quench your thirst for God. Nothing will come between you and your desire for Him. I pray your soul will be satisfied in heaven. My prayer over you is that you will forever be chasing after the things of God. That you will be grounded in Him and Him alone. Nothing else outside of God's great design will satisfy your soul. I pray if you ever feel lost or stranded, that your soul will return back to panting for God rapidly, in Jesus name, amen.

As a deer pants for flowing streams, so pants my soul for you, O God. Psalm 42:1

Affirmation: You will constantly chase after God.

God keeps His WORD

I pray that you have this scripture engraved on the tablet of your heart. That you will always remember that God is not man that He should ever lie or fail concerning His promises to you. He is not the son of man that He should repent or recant. I pray you will know with confidence that everything He has spoken concerning you, will come to pass. Knowing that what He has said He will do. What He has spoken, He will make it good. That you will remember that His promises and plan for you is already good and already done. I pray you will rest and in this assurance like never before. I am rooting for you and I pray you stay grounded in His promises, in Jesus name, amen.

God is not man, that He should lie, or a son of man, that He should change His mind. Has He said, and will He not do it? Or has He spoken, and will He not fulfill it? Numbers 23:19

Affirmation: You will trust wholeheartedly in God's words.

God's Goodness

I pray the overwhelming presence of God over you today according to His words. I pray your Father God Almighty will bless you and keep you. I pray the Lord will make His face shine upon you and be gracious to you. I pray He will lift up His countenance towards you and give you overwhelming peace. I pray when you call upon Him, He will turn His face and heart towards you and surround you with all you need. I pray He will overwhelm you with His love and His presence in every season and concerning all that pertains you, in Jesus name, amen.

The Lord bless you and keep you;
25 the Lord make his face to shine upon you and be gracious to you;
26 the Lord lift up his countenance upon you and give you peace. Numbers 6:24-26

Affirmation: You will walk in God's blessing, graciousness, and peace.

Enlarge me Oh Lord

Daddy God oooo #Sillyness. Lord Jesus, I pray over this child of Yours created in Your image and likeness. I pray that God will bless you indeed and enlarge your territory and that His hand will be with you. That God Almighty will keep you from all harm that you will not have pain. I pray over you that God is your shield and your covering from all evil known and unknown. I pray God will grant this request upon your life, in Jesus name, amen.

Jabez called upon the God of Israel, saying, "Oh that you would bless me and enlarge my border, and that your hand might be with me, and that you would keep me from harm so that it might not bring me pain!" And God granted what he asked. 1 Chronicles 4:10

Affirmation: Your territories and borders are enlarge.

Protection from ALL evil

I pray the Lord will protect you from all evil, harm, and dangers that you will ever encounter. I pray you will be preserved by God from all evil. God will preserve your soul – my dearest. He will guard your going out and your coming in from this time forth even forevermore. I speak over your life that you are protected in God. You will feel securely protected, surrounded, and affirmed in Him. I pray you will find solace in God as your ultimate protector, in Jesus name, amen.

The Lord will keep you from all evil; He will keep your life. [8] The Lord will keep your going out and your coming in from this time forth and forevermore. Psalm 121:7-8

Affirmation: You are shielded in God.

Request DONE

I am praying for you that as you ask it will be giving to you; as you seek, you will find; as you knock, the door will be open to you. For when you ask of Him, you will receive; when you seek Him out, you will find Him; and when you knock, the door will be open to you. Nothing great in this life will be out of your reach. You will be heard by God the moment you open your mouth. Your requests will constantly be before God and it will be granted. You will do great exploits here on earth for His name sake. Your desires will not be out of selfishness but for kingdom purposes and advancement, in Jesus name, amen.

"Ask, and it will be given to you; seek, and you will find; knock, and it will be opened to you. [8] For everyone who asks receives, and the one who seeks finds, and to the one who knocks it will be opened. Matthew 7:7-8

Affirmation: You will be sought out, heard, and found in God.

Keys of David

Hey my love, I pray that you know that God the Holy and True One has given you the key of David, that opens doors and no one can shut and shut doors no one can open. I pray you know that He sees your labor and work of love. That you see that He has set before you an open door that no one will ever be able to shut. Even in little, He sees your work and how you have diligently kept His word. He is rewarding you for your diligence and how you have kept His word and not denied His name. My God is diligently rewarding you in this hour for your faithfulness, steadfastness, consistency, for showing up, for not quitting, for making Him your priority – He is coming through for you in this moment, in Jesus name, amen.

"And to the angel of the church in Philadelphia write: 'The words of the Holy One, the True One, who has the key of David, who opens and no one will shut, who shuts and no one opens.

[8] "I know your works. Behold, I have set before you an open door, which no one is able to shut. I know that you have but little power, and yet you have kept My word and have not denied My name. Revelation 3:7-8

Affirmation: Doors will be open to you.

_____

_____

_____

_____

_____

_____

_____

_____

_____

_____

Strength

My prayer for you is that you will wait on the Lord today. I pray as you do, He shall renew your strength. You my love will mount up with wings like eagles. I pray you will run and not be weary. You will walk and not faint. I pray over you that you will not get tired in this hour. You will not faint, your strength will not fail you. I pray that as you walk in Him, you are receiving supernatural strength. You are receiving second wind to stay in this race and fight another day, in Jesus name, amen.

But they who wait for the Lord shall renew their strength; they shall mount up with wings like eagles; they shall run and not be weary; they shall walk and not faint. Isaiah 40:31

Affirmation: You are strengthened in the Lord.

God – Wealth Giver

Hey sweetie I am praying the word of God for you today. I pray that this day you shall remember the Lord your God, for it is He who gives you the power to get wealth. That He establishes His covenant which He swore to your fathers, as it is this day. I pray overflow and abundance for you. I pray you will always have more than you need. I pray you will seek and gain wealth in godly manner. I pray you will always operate in overflow and have more than enough. I pray you will use all that He's giving you to prosper the Kingdom of God. I pray you will understand and live out a life that shows that you are blessed to be a blessing to the people of God, in Jesus name, amen.

You shall remember the Lord your God, for it is he who gives you power to get wealth, that he may confirm his covenant that he swore to your fathers, as it is this day. Deuteronomy 8:18

Affirmation: You are strengthened in the Lord.

Mind & Heart Day

I pray that your mind, heart, and soul will fixate on the things that are true, honorable/noble, just/right, pure, lovely, commendable, excellent, and worthy of praise. I pray that your heart's cry will be focused on what God deems lovely, pure, excellent, and honorable. I pray your heart will not stray from these things. I pray these things will fill your heart and satisfy your soul. I pray your soul will crave what your Maker's desires for you, in Jesus name, amen.

Finally, brothers, whatever is true, whatever is honorable, whatever is just, whatever is pure, whatever is lovely, whatever is commendable, if there is any excellence, if there is anything worthy of praise, think about these things. Philippians 4:8

Affirmation: You will meditate on things honorable, pure, worthy of praise.

Faith & Virtue

My prayer for you is that you will make every effort to increase and add to your faith some virtue. I pray to virtue some knowledge; and to that self-control; to that steadfastness; to that some godliness, then brotherly affection, and to that more love. I pray these things will not depart from you. They will be embedded in your very being and character and in the existence of who you are. You will desire to be nothing but a person of noble and godly character all the days of your life in Him, in Jesus name, amen.

For this very reason, make every effort to supplement your faith with virtue, and virtue with knowledge, [6] and knowledge with self-control, and self-control with steadfastness, and steadfastness with godliness, [7] and godliness with brotherly affection, and brotherly affection with love. 2 Peter 1:5-7

Affirmation: You are a man of faith and virtue.

Discipline & Self-control

I pray that discipline will be the mantra of your daily existence – my dearest. I pray you will have the strength to discipline your body and keep it under control least after ministering to others, you are disqualified. I pray your profession of faith will attest to your lifestyle. I pray you will lead a life that glorifies God and not mock His name. I pray your life of discipline in prayer will stay steady in Christ. That you will live a life of utmost discipline before God in all areas of your live. Not a life of perfection but one wholly dedicated to the things of God and a heart like His, in Jesus name, amen.

But I discipline my body and keep it under control, lest after preaching to others I myself should be disqualified. 1 Corinthians 9:27

Affirmation: You are a man of discipline and self-control.

It is finished!!! You did we! We engaged numerous scriptures thirty-five times. Let's pray and seal all the prayer and work we have done in agreement in God.

Do you trust and believe God for all you have prayed for? I need you to meditate and memorize these scriptures below.

Therefore, I say to You, whatever things You ask when You pray, believe that You receive them, and You will have them. Mark 11:24

And since we have the same spirit of faith, according to what is written, "I believed and therefore I spoke," we also believe and therefore speak. 2 Corinthians 4:13

Why is this important?

I pray this has strengthened your faith. I pray that you will see the fruits of the seed you have planted either for yourself, your spouse, spouse to be. I pray this simple verse over you if you are still experiencing unbelief, "I believe but help my unbelief".

Lord, thank You for hearing us concerning Your promises for our lives, spouses, and others around us. We are grateful that You are a good God. All you do is great and perfect. We surrender it all to You in Your Son, Jesus Christ name, amen.

Have you thought about praying for your person? But ponder how to grow in this area with godly sincerity. This will help you ignite a fire and passion in you for God, yourself, your spouse, and your relationship. I pray you will begin to see the value and beauty in what He has ordained.

Made in the USA
Middletown, DE
23 December 2023

46731921R00056